Spotlight on

Fossils

Tim Wood

Franklin Watts

London · New York · Sydney · Toronto

© 1988 Franklin Watts

Franklin Watts
12a Golden Square
London W1

First published in the USA by
Franklin Watts Inc.
387 Park Avenue South
New York, N.Y. 10016

Franklin Watts Australia
14 Mars Road
Lane Cove
NSW 2066

Phototypeset by Keyspools
Limited
Printed in Hong Kong

UK ISBN: 0 86313 688 5

Illustrations:
Mike Atkinson
Jim Marks
Ralph Stobbart
Steve Wilson
Robert and Rhoda Burns

Photographs:
Imitor
British Antarctic Survey
Barnabys Picture Library
ZEFA

Design:
Janet King
Jim Marks

Technical consultant:
Dr Richard Moody

Note: A number of the
illustrations in this book originally
appeared in *Fossils*, A First Look
Book.

Contents

What are fossils?

Fossils are the preserved remains of prehistoric plants or animals. They tell us about life on Earth millions of years ago.

A fossil of the first bird, *Archaeopteryx.*

Fossils can be preserved in rock, ice
or tar, or in hardened tree sap
called amber. Most fossils are
formed from the hard parts of
animals, such as a skeleton or shell.
But the remains of soft-bodied
creatures or even footprints may
be found. 5

How fossils are formed

Most fossils are the remains of creatures which lived in water. Their remains sank to the sea or river bed and eventually became fossils. In time the water dried up, so rocks which were once under water became dry land. The wind and rain wear away the rock, revealing the fossils.

Fossil ammonites

Fossil formation

This ammonite, a relation of the squid, lived in the sea 150 million years ago.

When it died, its shell became buried under mud on the sea bed. The mud hardened into rock around the shell, forming a *fossil*.

Sometimes the shell may dissolve away, leaving *a hollow fossil mould*.

The mould may fill with mud or sand which turns to rock, forming *a fossil cast*.

What fossils can tell us

Fossils tell the story of the Earth. They tell us about animals and plants which are now extinct. They show us how animals and plants have changed and developed.

8 **A modern elephant with its ancient ancestor.**

One of the earliest fish.
Scientists have worked out
what it looked like from its
fossil remains.

Similar fossils have been found in
South America, Africa, India and
Australia. Scientists believe that
these land areas were once joined
together. Fossils can also tell
scientists what the climate on
Earth was like when that fossil,
plant or animal was alive.

The first fossils

The first fossils of living things are found in rocks about **3,500 million years old. Before that the Earth was a steaming hot ball of gas and dust. There was no oxygen, which animals need in order to live. Gradually, the Earth cooled.**

The Earth five thousand million years ago.

Lightning flashed and rain fell, forming pools of water. Tiny living cells grew in these pools. Over millions of years the cells developed into the first plants. Plants produce oxygen. As the amount of oxygen increased, the first animals appeared.

The time of ancient life

Rocks from the Palaeozoic era, 570 million years ago, contain the fossils of the first animals with hard skins or shells. Most of these animals lived in the sea and are now extinct.

Some Palaeozoic fossils

A trilobite. These died out, but the modern king crab is related to them.

A lampshell

At this time fishes, the first
animals with backbones, appeared.
Tiny plants began to grow on the
land. Gradually trees appeared
and developed into huge forests.
Many animals moved on to the
land in search of food. They
developed into amphibians and
reptiles.

The Age of Reptiles

The Age of Reptiles began about 225 million years ago in a time called the Mesozoic era. Great dinosaurs, like the *Supersaurus*, ruled the land. Some dinosaurs, such as the *Stegosaurus*, were armour-plated. Some, like the *Tyrannosaurus Rex*, were ferocious carnivores. Others, like the *Pterodactyl*, could fly.

Parasaurolophus, a crested dinosaur.

15

Life in the prehistoric seas

Towards the end of the Mesozoic era there were large areas of shallow sea. Marine dinosaurs, like the *Icthyosaurus* and the *Plesiosaurus*, hunted the fast swimming fishes which lived in these warm waters.

Ammonites were common in the Mesozoic seas. They are related to the octopus and squid.

Sea urchins, found in Mesozoic rocks, still live in the sea today.

Reptiles like these lived in Mesozoic seas.

Ichthyosaurus

A fossil Ichthyosaurus

Plesiosaurus

The marine dinosaurs had powerful fins which helped them to twist and turn in the water.

17

The Age of Mammals

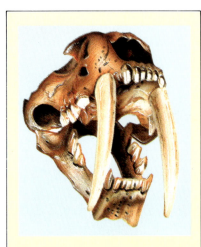

The fossil skull of a sabre-toothed cat showing its enormous front teeth.

About 65 million years ago, the dinosaurs died out. No one knows why they disappeared. They were replaced by mammals in a time called the Cenozoic era. We are living in that era today. Fossils show that there were many new plants and birds on Earth as well.

With no dinosaurs to challenge them, the new mammals spread over the Earth. Some became enormous. Gradually they developed into the familiar mammals we know today – dogs, cats, horses and elephants. The first human fossils are found in rocks five million years old.

This woolly mammoth was found almost perfectly preserved in the frozen soil of northern Russia.

Where to find fossils

Most fossils were formed under water, so it is best to hunt for them in rocks which were once under water. Sandstone, clay, shale and limestone are good rocks to choose.

Fossil-bearing cliffs.

Fossil hunters carefully digging up the fossils skeleton of a *Plesiosaurus*.

A special guide called a geological map will show you where these rocks can be found. Most rocks are buried under soil, so look for places where the soil has been removed. Cliffs, quarries and river banks are good places. You may need permission before starting to dig.

Collecting fossils

Useful tools for collecting fossils.

Choose a likely site from a geological map. Wear warm clothes and strong boots. Rocks, cliffs and quarries can be dangerous. Go with an adult and wear a helmet. You will need a hammer to break up rocks. Protect fossils in newspaper or boxes. Label them with the place and date of discovery.

The skeleton of a dinosaur, *Iguanodon*, built up from pieces of fossil bones.

Coal

Coal is a rock which can be burned as a fuel. It is the fossil remains of trees and plants which grew millions of years ago in swampy forests. Coal is usually found in layers called seams. These are sandwiched between layers of other rocks.

A coalmine.

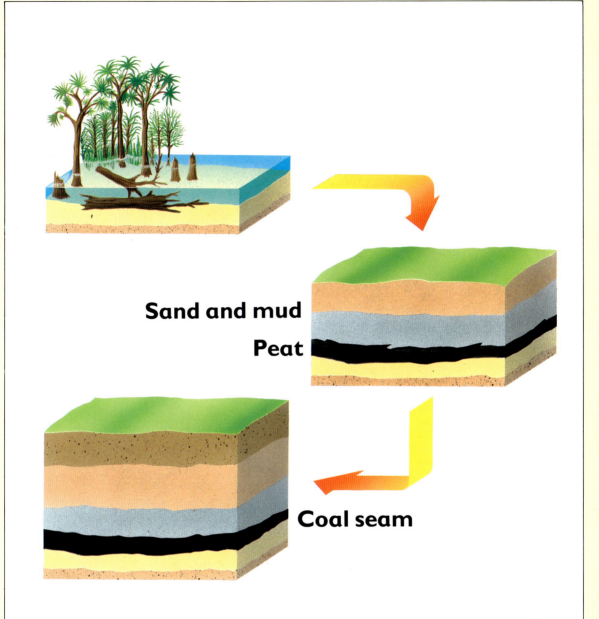

Sand and mud

Peat

Coal seam

Dead trees and plants fell into the swamps, forming thick layers of peat. Sometimes the sea flooded the forests. The water left behind sand and mud which hardened into rock. This pressed down on the peat, forming coal.

Oil and natural gas

Oil and natural gas are also fossil fuels. They are formed from the bodies of countless tiny plants and animals which lived in warm seas.

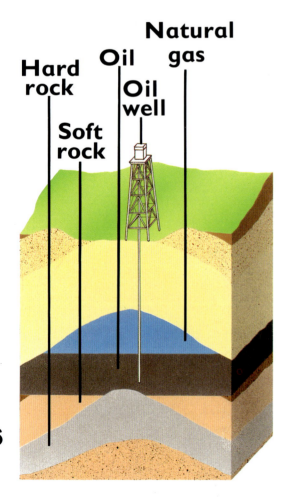

Hard rock

Soft rock

Oil

Oil well

Natural gas

Oil and gas collect in pockets in soft rocks between layers of very hard rocks. Holes are drilled and then the oil or gas is pumped up to the surface.

An oil rig in the sea.

Oil or gas is often found under the sea bed. Oil rigs are used to drill down into the rock. The oil or gas is pumped along a pipeline to the shore.

The fossil record

Millions of years ago	Period	Meaning	
2–Present 65–2	Quaternary Tertiary	The fourth formation The third formation	
136–65	Cretaceous	Chalky	
190–136	Jurassic	After the Jura mountains	
225–190	Triassic	The rocks can be divided into three groups	
280–225	Permian	After a town in Russia	
345–280	Carboniferous	Coal bearing	
395–345	Devonian	After the county of Devon	
430–395	Silurian	After an ancient Welsh tribe	
500–430	Ordovician	After another Welsh tribe	
570–500	Cambrian	After the Latin name of Wales	
4,500–570	Precambrian	Before the Cambrian	

Scientists compare fossils from different times and places to make a record of life on Earth.

Animals and plants	Era
The age of humans. Many mammals, birds and flowering plants emerge, as well as new animals without backbones.	Cenozoic
The flowering plants appear while many groups of animals, including the dinosaurs, become extinct. Giant ferns dominate the plant life. Dinosaurs rule the land and the first bird appears. The first dinosaurs and mammals appear.	Mesozoic
New reptiles and plants appear on land. Many ammonites swim in the seas. The first land animals—reptiles—appear. Much of the land is covered in swampy forests. Plants cover the land and the first forests grow. Animals, called amphibians, appear which live part of their life on land. The first land plants appear. The seas contain many different fishes and huge sea scorpions. Sea-living plants and animals, including brachiopods, trilobites, graptolites and the first fishes. Sea-living plants and animals, such as jellyfish, sponges, corals and trilobites.	Palaeozoic
First simple creatures appeared 3,500 million years ago.	Precambrian

Fossil facts

Fossils of the first-known animals were found in Australia. Some are of jellyfish as big as truck wheels!

The first-known life on Earth is over three thousand million years old. Fossils of tiny cells were found in a type of rock in South Africa. These cells were so small that hundreds would have fitted on the full stop at the end of this sentence.

The largest fossil insect ever found lived in the Carboniferous Period. It was a dragonfly called *Meganeura*, with a wingspan of 60 cm (2 ft).

There is a Dinosaur National Monument in Utah, USA. This is a wall, 58 metres long, which has more than a thousand dinosaur bones embedded in it. Since 1909, scientists have collected vast numbers of fossils. Millions of years ago, the wall was part of a sandy river bed in which dinosaurs became stuck and died.

The largest dinosaur egg ever found was discovered in France. It was the size of a football!

The town of Artesia in Colorado, USA, changed its name to Dinosaur because so many dinosaur fossils were found nearby! Even the streets are named after dinosaurs.

Living fossils is a term which refers to animals and plants that have remained almost unchanged for millions of years. the most famous living fossil is a fish called the coelacanth. It was thought to be extinct, until one was caught alive off the coast of South Africa in 1938.

Glossary

Here is the meaning of some of the words used in this book:

Amphibians

Animals which are able to live on land and in water.

Era

A period of history.

Extinct

This word is used to describe groups of animals or plants which have died out completely.

Geologist

Someone who studies the Earth's rocks and soil

Palaeontologist

Someone who studies the fossil remains of plants, animals and human beings.

Limestone

A type of rock formed, usually in the sea, from the shells of sea creatures which have broken up and fallen to the sea bed.

Mammals

Warm-blooded animals which feed their babies with their own milk. ("Warm-blooded" means that these animals are able to control their own body heat.)

Mould

A hollow shape formed when the hard skeleton or shell of an animal is dissolved away inside a rock.

Peat

A brown substance formed from the remains of dead trees and plants.

Prehistoric

Before written records were kept.

Reptiles

Cold-blooded animals that creep or crawl. ("Cold-blooded" means that these animals need to be warmed by the heat of the sun.)

31

Index